Taco Table

Lois Ellen Frank

WESTERN NATIONAL PARKS ASSOCIATION
TUCSON, ARIZONA

Acknowledgments

This book is dedicated to my husband, Sean; to everyone in my family, all of whom love to eat and experiment with cooking and trying new recipes; and to all of the wonderful cooks and chefs who helped create and make up the taco table.

I would like to thank the following people for their help in making this book possible: Noé Cano, the kitchen manager and sous chef at the Santa Fe School of Cooking, who is originally from Chacaltianguis in Veracruz, Mexico; and Alma Aguirre-Loya, a home cook originally from Chihuahua, Mexico, who is studying to be a professional chef at the Santa Fe Community College culinary arts program. Both were instrumental in teaching me the fundamentals of traditional taco making. They helped me to understand the importance of making tortillas from scratch. Fresh tortillas with every taco meal are part of what makes the meal so delicious.

Thanks also to Walter Whitewater, a Native American chef from the Diné (Navajo) Nation and my chef de cuisine at Red Mesa, for working with me on creating, testing, and tasting the Native American influenced recipes that are a part of this book. I would like to thank all of the chefs and cooks who have inspired me to make great food, to have fun while doing it, and to experiment and create new dishes. I would also like to thank Abby Mogollón, my editor, for doing such a fantastic job on the text, and Nancy Campana, the designer, for making the book look so beautiful. Thanks to Derek Gallagher and everyone at WNPA for making this book possible. Finally, thanks to all of the farmers and food producers who provide clean and good food. Their commitment helps me create delicious, wholesome recipes and meals. Thank you.

Cover photograph from Bison Meat Navajo Tacos, page 19.

Receive a free Western National Parks Association catalogue, featuring hundreds of publications.
Email: info@wnpa.org or visit www.wnpa.org for our online store.

Written by Lois Ellen Frank
Edited by Abby Mogollón
Design by Campana Design
Photography by Lois Ellen Frank
Printing by Imago
Printed in China

Contents

Taco History

Comida! One mouthwatering word sums up southwestern cuisine. Corn, beans, and chiles from indigenous cultures; wheat, beef, and cheese from the Spanish colonization of the region. All of this enhanced and enriched by cooks from the many cultures this area embraces. And what is more emblematic of this food than the taco? Beans and beef, cheese and chiles nestled in a wrapping of freshly cooked corn or wheat flour.

Tacos have formed the basis of southwestern meals for thousands of years and are a hallmark of the region's contemporary cuisine. When the Spanish first arrived in Mexico, the indigenous people were eating colored corn tortillas, which they called *tlaxcalpacholi,* an Aztec Nahuatl word. The Spanish renamed these handmade grain wraps "tortillas," and "taco" became the name for the tortilla with its filling.

Bernal Díaz del Castillo (1496–1584) witnessed the first Spanish taco feast when he visited the lake region in the Valley of Mexico nearly 500 years ago. He described people eating a tortilla filled with small fish. Hernán Cortés, a Spanish colonizer, had arranged the feast for his captains during their first expedition.

The word *taco* could be compared to the word *sandwich* in English. What varies with tacos are the contents, or the ingredients, inside the taco. Fillings reflect the region in which they are made. For example, in coastal areas, you will find tacos filled with fish and seafood, while in the interior, meat fillings are more common. Tacos can contain practically any type of filling, not only meat and seafood, but poultry, vegetables, and cheese. People usually eat them by hand, with salsa or vegetables such as onion, cilantro, lettuce, or cabbage. The ingredients of a taco are limited only by the contents of a cook's refrigerator and imagination.

Traditional Mexican tacos are normally served on flat tortillas that have been warmed or cooked on a *comal,* a clay or cast-iron griddle. *Comal* originates from the Nahuatl word *comalli.* Comal cooking is usually done over an open flame, but comales can be found in modern kitchens today as part of the stove top. Because the tortillas served with traditional Mexican tacos are soft, they can be folded over or pinched together and eaten without utensils.

Tacos can be a snack or a meal; however, it is much more common to see tacos being eaten in the morning or as a nighttime snack than as the main midday meal. Permanent *puestos* (stalls) and storefront *taquerías* sell tacos throughout Mexico.

Tacos are a fun food to make and eat. Because you eat them with your hands, they are a comfortable and welcoming food that each family member, friend, or guest can make specifically to his or her own liking. I have had so much fun learning about and preparing tacos for this book that they have become a major part of my diet. The best way to understand tacos is to plan a taco menu, pick your favorite salsas to go with them, make your tortillas, and then have fun assembling them. You will find it easy to prepare a delicious meal starting with the taco.

Tacos are a food that brings people and families together; they create a taco table that is nutritious, healthy, and warming to the soul. What follows in this book are my versions of tacos that originated in Mexico. Each recipe has a piece of ancient Mexico and a piece of myself in it. The recipes are easy to make and delicious to eat. I recommend you use my recipes as a starting point and develop versions that become your own. In the process you will create your own taco table.

NOTE: I like to start with whole spices in all of my recipes. The flavors are much more pungent and savory. In place of powdered spices, you can use whole coriander seeds, cumin seeds, and peppercorns, grinding them to a powder in a spice or coffee grinder. Use two coffee grinders: one for whole-bean coffee and the other for spices.

Sustainable Food Selection

We are in a time in history when buying good, clean food for which growers are fairly paid is a conscious choice that we can make. Where we buy our food dictates food policy and programs that ultimately affect all of us. I choose to buy local, organic, and fair trade food products whenever possible. The food tastes better, and I know it didn't travel a long distance to get to my table. I buy foods from distant places—such as coffee, quinoa, avocados, and shrimp—from sustainable sources that support cooperative and community efforts.

Our National Parks

Our nation's national parks and heritage areas are laboratories for sustainable practice. These special places offer demonstration gardens and historic ranches, and they provide wonderful links to locally grown and produced products and goods.

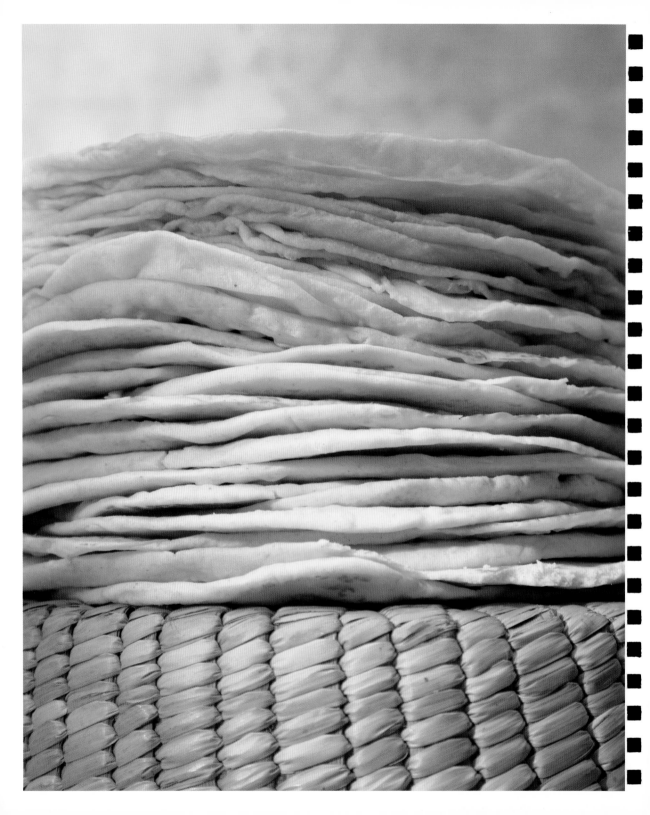

Homemade Tortillas

Corn, Wheat & Mesquite

Tortillas de Maís
Corn Tortillas

Corn tortillas are available in most supermarkets today and are certainly an option, but I would encourage you to make your own homemade corn tortillas, even if only once. As soon as you've held the dough in your hands, placed it onto a comal or skillet, and made it into a fresh corn tortilla, you are sure to be a convert. I didn't grow up with homemade corn tortillas, so at first making them from scratch seemed a bit foreign to me. As soon as I realized how easy it was to do, how delicious the tortillas were to eat, and how much I enjoyed the process, I started making my own. Now, I always make my corn tortillas. My friends Alma Aguirre-Loya and Noé Cano grew up in Mexico with mothers who made tortillas every day. Alma continues to make tortillas daily for her children, and Noé teaches tortilla making at the Santa Fe School of Cooking.

2 cups corn *masa*
1 teaspoon kosher salt
2 cups warm water

In a medium-sized mixing bowl, combine the corn flour, salt, and water and mix together until you have formed a soft dough. You can do this with a spoon, but I prefer to use my hands. After the corn flour and water are completely mixed, form balls just smaller than a golf ball with your hands. Set aside.

Preheat your comal or cast-iron skillet so that it is very hot.

Place one ball in the center of a tortilla press and press together to make one corn tortilla. I place the corn masa ball inside a plastic bag that I cut in half, leaving a seam on one side, so that the dough doesn't stick to the tortilla press.

Remove the tortilla from the press and plastic and place it on the comal. Cook the first side of the tortilla for 10 to 15 seconds, then turn it over and cook for approximately 30 to 40 seconds. Turn it over again and cook until it puffs. That's when the tortilla is done.

Place the cooked tortilla in a kitchen towel inside a basket or bowl and prepare the next tortilla. Stack the tortillas on top of one another so that they keep warm.

Serve warm with your favorite taco filling and salsa.

Blue Corn Flour Tortillas

Blue corn flour tortillas are made from dried Native American blue corn that is ground into a fine flour, unlike meal which is coarse and grainy. Blue corn flour is used in a variety of traditional food dishes. It is sweeter and nuttier tasting than other types of corn flours, such as yellow or white. Blue corn flour can be found in most supermarkets or specialty food stores throughout the Southwest.

1 cup blue corn flour
2 cups organic all-purpose flour

1 teaspoon salt
1 cup warm water

In a medium-sized mixing bowl combine dry ingredients, then slowly mix in warm water until a soft dough forms. You can do this with a spoon, but I always use my hands. With your hands, shape the dough into balls just smaller than a golf ball and set aside.

Preheat your comal or cast-iron skillet until hot.

Place one ball in the center of a tortilla press and press together to make one tortilla. I use a plastic sandwich bag that I cut in half, leaving a seam on one side so that I can place the masa ball inside the plastic. This keeps the dough from sticking to the tortilla press.

Remove the tortilla from the press and the plastic and place it on the comal. Cook the first side of the tortilla for 10 to 15 seconds, then turn it over and cook for approximately 30 to 40 seconds. Turn it over again. The tortilla is done when it puffs.

Place the cooked tortilla in a kitchen towel inside a basket or bowl and prepare the next tortilla. Stack the tortillas on top of one another to keep them warm.

Serve warm with your favorite taco filling and salsa.

Tortillas de Harina
Flour Tortillas

This easy recipe makes delicious flour tortillas that everyone will enjoy. There are other variations and many different ways to make flour tortillas, but this recipe is my favorite because of the texture of the tortilla. These five simple ingredients come together in a perfect dough.

2 cups unbleached flour
½ teaspoon kosher salt
1 teaspoon baking powder

⅓ cup lard or shortening
1 cup warm water

Mix dry ingredients together. Fold in the lard. Then slowly add the water and mix together thoroughly. Using your hands on a lightly floured cutting board, knead the dough mixture for 3 to 5 minutes until you can stick your finger into the center and no dough sticks to it. If the dough is too moist add additional flour.

Let the dough rest at room temperature for 30 minutes in a covered bowl.

After the dough has rested, form small portions into golf ball–sized balls. Place a ball in a large tortilla press and press into a tortilla between two sheets of a cut plastic bag. You can also roll out each tortilla with a rolling pin or pat them out by hand. Each tortilla should be approximately 6 to 8 inches in diameter and about ⅛ inch thick.

Heat a cast-iron pan or griddle to medium to high heat then place the tortilla on it. Cook until you see bubbles or a few brown spots. Turn it over and cook until done. Remove from the heat and place in a basket or bowl lined with a cloth napkin to keep warm while you make the remainder of the tortillas.

Serve warm with your favorite taco filling and salsa.

Indian Fry Bread & Tortilla Bread

This recipe can be fried for Indian tacos or used for a tortilla bread that is cooked on a comal. Both versions work well with Bison Meat Navajo Tacos (page 19) but are delicious with any of the tacos in this book.

4 cups organic unbleached flour
2 tablespoons baking powder
¼ cup vegetable shortening or lard

1 teaspoon kosher salt
1½ cups warm water
3 cups vegetable shortening for frying

In a medium-sized mixing bowl combine flour, baking powder, lard or shortening and kosher salt. Gradually stir in the water until the dough becomes soft and pliable without sticking to the bowl. Knead the dough on a lightly floured cutting board or surface for 4 minutes, repeatedly folding the outer edges of the dough toward the center. Return the dough to the bowl, cover with plastic wrap, and let rise for 30 minutes.

Shape the dough into small-sized balls and roll out to ¼-inch thickness on a lightly floured surface using a rolling pin or your hands. I always use my hands, which create slightly uneven breads, but everyone knows they were handmade. I think it gives each taco a little character. Stretch or roll the dough to about 8 to 10 inches in diameter.

For fry bread, melt the 3 cups of vegetable shortening in a skillet or wide saucepan. I prefer a saucepan because it prevents the oil from splattering. The oil should be hot but not smoking. Place your shaped dough circle into the hot oil, slipping it in gently to avoid splattering. Cook until the dough turns golden brown and puffs. Turn over with 2 forks or a pair of tongs and cook until both sides are golden brown. Remove from the pan and drain on paper towels until the excess oil is absorbed. While you fry the rest of the batch, keep finished breads warm between two clean kitchen towels.

For tortilla bread, prepare the dough in exactly the same way but do not fry it. Instead, heat a cast-iron skillet or griddle until very hot, place dough onto skillet and cook 2 to 3 minutes on each side until it browns. Keep breads warm between two clean kitchen towels.

Serve immediately with your favorite taco topping.

Mesquite Flour Tortillas

Mesquite meal is a traditional Native American food that is produced by gathering ripened seedpods from the mesquite tree. The seedpods are ground into a high-protein flour that has a caramel-like flavor and is a good source of calcium, manganese, potassium, iron, and zinc. It is also high in fiber and has been known to stabilize blood sugar levels. Plus, it is delicious in tortillas.

Mesquite meal flour can be purchased from several sources, but I always buy the meal from Native Seeds/SEARCH, a nonprofit conservation organization based in Tucson, Arizona. The group conserves, distributes, and documents the adapted and diverse varieties of agricultural seeds and their wild relatives and the role these seeds play in cultures of the American Southwest and northwest Mexico.

2 cups all-purpose flour
½ cup mesquite meal flour
½ teaspoon baking powder

½ cup vegetable shortening
1½ cups warm water

Mix together the dry ingredients in a medium-sized mixing bowl. Add the vegetable shortening and mix together using a slotted spoon. Slowly add the warm water, mixing with the slotted spoon, until dough is soft and pliable. Knead the dough on a floured work surface for 3 to 4 minutes, just until it is very soft and pliable and doesn't stick to your hands.

Cover the dough with plastic wrap and let it rest for 20 minutes. Remove the plastic wrap and on a lightly floured work surface form the dough into small balls the size of a golf ball.

Heat a cast-iron skillet or comal until very hot. Using a rolling pin, roll out each dough ball to approximately 8 inches in diameter. Place the tortilla onto the cast-iron skillet or comal and cook until it bubbles, then flip the tortilla and cook the other side for the same amount of time.

Place cooked tortillas in a basket lined with a soft cloth or towel to keep them warm while you finish the batch.

Serve with your favorite taco filling and salsa.

Meat

Beef, Bison, Lamb & Pork Tacos

Tacos Alambrados
Beef Tacos

This is a rich meat taco that is dressed up with oyster mushrooms and bell peppers. I prefer it with flour tortillas, but it can also be eaten with homemade corn tortillas. It is made with beef tenderloin, which is, in my opinion, one of the most tender and best-tasting beef cuts you can buy. I like these tacos with Salsa de Oregano Mexicano (page 55) or Salsa Borracho (page 55).

1½ pounds beef tenderloin, trimmed and cut into
    1-inch cubes
1 serrano chile, seeds and stems removed,
    finely chopped
½ teaspoon garlic powder
½ teaspoon kosher salt
½ teaspoon black pepper, ground
1 tablespoon olive oil

1½ cups oyster mushrooms, sliced
½ orange bell pepper, chopped
½ yellow bell pepper, chopped
½ green bell pepper, chopped
1 red onion, chopped
18–24 slices queso asadero
Flour tortillas

Combine serrano chile, garlic powder, kosher salt, and black pepper in a medium-sized mixing bowl. Add the meat cubes and mix thoroughly, making sure each piece of meat is coated with the spice mixture.

In a cast-iron skillet or frying pan, heat olive oil over medium to high heat until hot but not smoking. Add the meat and stir constantly for

1 to 2 minutes until meat starts to brown. Add the mushrooms, bell peppers, and onion and sauté for 5 minutes until the vegetables are soft. Remove from heat.

Place in a flour tortilla with three slices of asadero cheese and serve immediately with your favorite salsa.

Tacos de los Niños
Ground Beef Tacos

I call this recipe the Tacos de los Niños, or children's tacos, because children devour them. My friend Alma helped me test many of these recipes, and this one was her daughters' favorite. The girls said they loved the texture of the ground beef with the lettuce, tomato, and cheddar cheese on top. It is perfect for kids because it has no chile; however, if you have a spicier palate, add a pinch of ground New Mexico red chile powder for a little heat and some extra flavor. This taco can be served in either a soft corn tortilla or a hard corn tortilla that has been fried.

1 tablespoon olive oil
1¼ pounds ground beef, with 15 percent fat
    content
2 cloves garlic, minced
1/3 cup white onion, chopped
1/8 teaspoon cumin, finely ground
½ teaspoon kosher salt
½ teaspoon black pepper, finely ground

1 teaspoon New Mexico red chile powder
    (optional)
Corn tortillas or taco shells
¾ cup cheddar cheese, shredded
1 cup lettuce, shredded
½ cup Roma tomatoes, diced
Sour cream (optional)

In a cast-iron skillet or frying pan, heat olive oil over medium heat. Add the ground beef and cook for approximately 4 minutes. As the meat cooks, use a slotted spoon or a potato masher to separate the ground beef into small pieces. Add the garlic, stir for 1 minute, and then add the onion. Cook for 3 minutes, stirring constantly to prevent burning. Add the cumin, kosher salt, black pepper, and chile powder (if desired).

Cook for another 2 minutes until the meat is completely done. Remove from heat.

To make each taco, place some of the ground beef mixture inside each corn tortilla or taco shell, top with the cheddar cheese, lettuce, and tomato.

Top with a dab of sour cream, if you wish.

Tacos de Carne Asada
Cowboy Tacos

This recipe was taught to me by Alma Aguirre-Loya, who is originally from northern Mexico, where ranching is a way of life. I call these tacos "cowboy tacos" because they are a very simple and delicious meat taco. For this dish, Alma asks her butcher to thinly slice the skirt steak partway through, leaving it in a whole piece. Almost like buying sliced meat from a deli! In some supermarkets or meat markets, this type of meat is referred to as *carne ranchera*. I had never cooked meat this way before, but I fell in love with the flavor and method of preparing these tacos after I learned how to make them. I think you will too!

1½ pounds carne ranchera (skirt steak), very thinly sliced
¾ teaspoon kosher salt
¾ teaspoon black pepper, ground
1 cup lettuce, shredded (optional)

Season the thinly sliced skirt steak on both sides with the salt and black pepper. Set aside while you heat a cast-iron skillet until hot but not smoking. (If you prefer, you can use a grill.) Place meat in the skillet or on the grill and cook for 3 minutes, then turn over with kitchen tongs and cook for another 3 minutes. Remove from heat and cut first into strips, and then into ½-inch squares. Serve immediately with your favorite tortillas and salsa. My favorite salsa with these meat tacos is the Chipotle Salsa (page 54).

Bison Meat Navajo Tacos

This recipe is a variation on the famous Indian tacos that are served at many ceremonial powwows, arts and craft festivals, rodeos, and Pueblo Feast Days. Walter Whitewater, a Diné (Navajo) chef, and I came up with this delicious Indian taco variation. We make our fry bread taco bottoms smaller and create a healthy topping for the taco with organically raised bison meat, organic cooked pinto and kidney beans, local organic baby lettuce greens, heirloom tomatoes, and avocado.

Taco meat:
2 tablespoons olive oil
1 pound organic ground bison meat
1 medium onion, diced
6 cloves garlic, minced
2 fresh tomatoes, coarsely chopped
2 cups pinto beans, cooked (fresh or canned)
1 cup kidney beans, cooked (fresh or canned)
1 tablespoon New Mexico mild red chile powder, ground
1 teaspoon kosher salt

Taco topping:
2 cups organic baby greens, washed and chopped
1 tomato, finely diced
1 8-oz package or 2 cups cheddar cheese, grated
¼ cup New Mexico or Anaheim green chiles, roasted and peeled, stems removed, and chopped (see page 62 for preparation instructions)
1 ripe avocado
Fry bread

In a cast-iron skillet or frying pan, heat the olive oil until hot. Add the ground bison meat and use a slotted spoon or potato masher to break the meat into small pieces as it cooks. Cook until completely brown, stirring to prevent burning, for approximately 5 minutes.

Add the onion and garlic and cook for another 3 to 4 minutes, until the onion is soft and clear. Add the tomatoes and cook for another 3 minutes, stirring constantly to prevent burning. Add the cooked pinto and kidney beans and stir. Add the

New Mexico red chile powder and salt and stir again. Let cook for an additional minute, stirring to prevent burning.

Remove from heat. Spoon the meat-and-bean mixture on top of a freshly made fry bread, then top with a portion of the baby greens, tomato, grated cheddar cheese, chopped green chiles, and avocado.

Serve immediately.

Lamb Kabob Tacos

This taco recipe is a favorite of my husband's and very simple to make. Lamb is a tender meat and has a delicious mild flavor from the grasses that the lambs graze on. I buy organic lamb meat from Shepherd's Lamb at the Santa Fe Farmer's Market. On their farm, proprietors Antonio and Molly Manzanares raise some of the best-tasting lamb I have ever eaten. See the Sources (page 64) for contact information. Or look into organic lamb meat where you live. You will notice a huge difference in taste. I like to serve these tacos with Pico de Gallo Salsa (page 54), which adds a zing of fresh flavor.

1 lb. lamb kabobs (lamb shoulder), cut into ½-inch cubes
2 tablespoons New Mexico or Anaheim red chile powder
½ teaspoon chipotle chile powder
1 teaspoon kosher salt
2 tablespoons olive oil
½ medium onion, cut into strips
2 Roma tomatoes, coarsely cut
Flour tortillas

In a medium-sized mixing bowl, combine red chile powder, chipotle chile powder, and salt. Dredge cubed meat into mixture until all meat is completely coated. Set aside.

Over medium to high heat, heat 1 tablespoon olive oil in a cast-iron pan or skillet until hot but not smoking. Add the onion and sauté for 3 minutes, stirring to prevent burning. Add tomatoes and sauté for another 3 minutes stirring constantly. Remove from heat and set aside.

In a separate cast-iron pan or skillet, heat the remaining tablespoon of olive oil until hot but not smoking. Add the meat and cook for 3 minutes until meat is cooked as desired, stirring to prevent the meat from burning and to ensure that it cooks evenly. I prefer my meat medium rare to medium for the best taste and greatest tenderness, but add 1 to 2 minutes of cooking time if you prefer your meat a little more done.

Add the cooked onions and tomatoes and cook for 1 additional minute. Serve immediately with flour tortillas and Pico de Gallo or other salsa.

Tacos al Pastor
Shepherd's-Style Tacos

Tacos al pastor are very popular in Mexico. These flavorful tacos are made of spiced pork that is usually cut into slivers and served with a salsa. They are thought to be a Mexican adaptation of the spit-grilled meat brought to Mexico by immigrants from Lebanon. I have modified the traditional recipe for the perfect blend of spices and pork. I recommend the Salsa de Piña (page 56) for this taco, as the sweetness of the pineapple pairs perfectly with the chile marinade.

For the marinade:
2 whole dried chiles de pasilla, seeded and stemmed
1 whole dried chile guajillo, seeded and stemmed
½ onion, coarsely chopped
3 tablespoons organic apple cider vinegar
2 tablespoons water
½ teaspoon salt
¼ teaspoon black pepper, ground

Taco meat:
1¼ pounds pork loin, cubed into ¼- to ½-inch pieces, trim off fat
2 tablespoons olive oil
Corn or flour tortillas

Begin by preparing the marinade. Remove the seeds and stems from each dried chile and tear them into small pieces. Blend all the marinade ingredients and the chile pieces in a blender until smooth, approximately 2 to 3 minutes.

In a medium-sized mixing bowl, combine the cubed pork meat with the marinade. Stir the meat until completely coated. Cover the bowl with plastic wrap and refrigerate for at least one hour and as long as overnight.

In a cast-iron skillet or stainless steel sauté pan, heat olive oil over medium to high heat. Cook the marinated pork thoroughly, approximately 4 to 5 minutes.

Remove from heat. Serve immediately with either corn or flour tortillas and salsa.

Shredded Pork Tacos

Makes 6 to 8 tacos

This recipe uses pork that is shredded, giving a wonderful texture to the tacos and making the meat tender and soft. Toasting the herbs before they are used to season the pork adds flavor and depth to the filling. Mixing the shredded meat with the New Mexico Red Chile Sauce is a must, as it provides the spicy final flavoring.

2 bay leaves
¼ teaspoon whole black peppercorns
¼ teaspoon whole cloves
¼ teaspoon whole coriander seeds
1 teaspoon kosher salt

1½ pounds pork shoulder, cut into large 3-inch cubes
1 clove garlic, sliced
5 cups water
Corn or flour tortillas

Heat a small saucepan over high heat until it is very hot. Add the bay leaves, peppercorns, cloves, and coriander seeds. Toast for 1 minute, until the spices turn a light brown, stirring constantly with a spoon to prevent burning. Remove from heat and set aside.

In a large pot, bring 5 cups of water to boil over high heat. Add the toasted spices, salt, garlic, and pork.

Bring to a boil, then reduce the heat and simmer for 45 minutes, skimming off and discarding the fat and foam on the top every 5 to 10 minutes. When fully cooked, the pork meat should fall apart to the touch.

Remove the meat from the heat, drain the liquid, and let cool. After the pork has cooled, shred it into small pieces with your fingers and set aside.

New Mexico Red Chile sauce:

2 tablespoons olive oil
½ large or 1 medium onion, chopped
1 teaspoon minced garlic
1 teaspoon coriander seed, finely ground

½ teaspoon black pepper, ground
¼ teaspoon cumin, finely ground
1 teaspoon apple cider vinegar
⅓ cup New Mexico or Anaheim red chile powder
2 cups chicken broth

In a saucepan, heat olive oil until hot but not smoking. Add chopped onion and cook 1 minute, stirring to prevent burning. Add garlic, coriander, pepper, and cumin and sauté 1 minute. Add the apple cider vinegar and red chile powder and stir constantly to prevent burning for 1 minute. Add the

chicken broth and stir until combined. Increase the heat and bring to a boil, then reduce and cook for 10 minutes, stirring to prevent burning.

Combine the shredded pork with the New Mexico Red Chile Sauce, reheat, and serve immediately with either corn or flour tortillas.

Poultry

Turkey, Chicken & Egg Tacos

Tacos de Pavo
Turkey Breast Tacos

These healthy and quick tacos are a nice way to use turkey breast. Look for all-natural, hormone-free, organic turkey products. The recipe works well with chicken breasts, too. I make these tacos with my favorite green chile sauce, which comes from the Garcia family in Portales, New Mexico. The family has made New Mexico–style salsas and sauces for more than a century, and they have been sharing them with consumers since 1975. Try this brand or use another locally made green chile for these tacos. I like to eat this taco dish with large flour tortillas rolled up on the ends burrito-style, which holds in the delicious juices and green chile sauce.

1 tablespoon olive oil
1 medium yellow onion, cut in half then thinly
    sliced
4 tomatoes, coarsely chopped
2 cloves garlic, minced

1¼ pounds natural turkey or chicken breast, cut
    into ½-inch by 3-inch strips
½ cup of jarred green chile sauce
Flour tortillas

In a cast-iron skillet or frying pan, heat olive oil and sauté onions for 3 to 4 minutes until they start to turn brown and crystallize. Stir occasionally to prevent burning. Add the tomatoes and cook for an additional minute, stirring constantly. Add the garlic and stir again. Cook for 2 minutes, then add the turkey or chicken breast strips, and cook for an additional 3 to 5 minutes until the meat is completely cooked. Add the green chile sauce and sauté for 2 to 3 minutes.

Serve immediately.

Tacos de Pollo
Chicken Breast Tacos

This easy recipe is both nutritious and delicious. Chicken is a versatile meat that is perfect for tacos. As with most foods, the better the quality of the chicken, the better your tacos will taste. I get my chicken from a CSA (community supported agriculture) that raises organic chicken. Preparing and cooking the chicken for the tacos takes just minutes, so I always decide what salsa I will be serving with my chicken tacos ahead of time and make the salsa first. This way, I can serve the tacos as soon as the chicken is ready. For this recipe, I like Salsa Verde (page 57).

1 tablespoon olive oil
1½ pounds chicken breast, boneless and skinless, cut into small pieces about ½-inch square

1 teaspoon kosher salt
¼ teaspoon black pepper, ground
Corn or flour tortillas

In a cast-iron skillet or stainless steel frying pan, heat olive oil until hot but not smoking. Season the chicken with salt and pepper. Add the cut chicken pieces and sauté over medium-high heat until completely cooked, approximately 5 minutes. Stir to prevent burning.

Remove from heat and serve with your favorite salsa. I recommend the Salsa Verde (page 57) made from tomatillos, cilantro, and jalapeño chiles.

Serve with either corn or flour tortillas.

Pollo al Carbón
Chicken Fajita Tacos

These tacos are a sure bet: easy to make and absolutely delicious. The fajita taco can be found in many restaurants in the United States. In Mexico the same taco might be called *al carbón*, meaning meat that is cooked quickly on a hot grill to retain its flavor and moistness. The sautéed vegetables accompanying the meat add a sweet flavor, nice texture, and pleasing color to the dish. If you don't have a spicy palate, add less of the chipotle chile or omit it altogether.

1 medium red onion, cut in half then sliced
5 cloves garlic, finely chopped
1 green bell pepper, thinly sliced
½ yellow bell pepper, thinly sliced
½ red bell pepper, thinly sliced
4 tomatoes, chopped
1¼ pounds boneless, skinless chicken breast, fat removed, cut into 1-inch by 3-inch strips

3 tablespoons olive oil
1 teaspoon kosher salt
½ teaspoon black pepper, ground
1½ teaspoons chipotle seasoning (see Southwest Pantry page 60)
Flour tortillas

In a cast-iron skillet or frying pan, heat 1 tablespoon olive oil until hot but not smoking. Add sliced onion and cook for 1 minute, stirring constantly. Add the garlic, stir, and then add the three colors of sliced bell peppers and cook until soft, approximately 2 to 3 minutes. Add tomatoes, stir again, then remove from heat and set aside.

In a mixing bowl, combine chicken strips with kosher salt, black pepper, and chipotle seasoning. Dredge meat in the spices until the chicken is completely coated.

In another skillet, over medium to high heat, heat the remaining 2 tablespoons of olive oil until hot but not smoking. Cook the chicken strips for 4 to 5 minutes, stirring constantly to prevent burning and to ensure that the meat cooks evenly and thoroughly.

Remove from heat.

Serve immediately with the sautéed vegetables. I recommend serving this dish with homemade flour tortillas and your favorite salsa.

Chicken Pibil Tacos

Makes 6 to 8 tacos

This recipe was taught to me by Veracruz native Noe Cano, one of the chefs I work with at the Santa Fe School of Cooking. It is a delicious way to incorporate organic, boneless chicken breast into a taco dish. The term *pibil* comes from a slow-roasting technique, originating not in Veracruz but in the Yucatan. It is a lovely illustration of the dynamic way that recipes are adapted and reinterpreted throughout Mexico. This recipe speeds up the slow-cooking process but ends in the same way—with tender shredded meat. The secret ingredient is the Salsa de Pibil (page 56). This spicy and robust salsa is a perfect match for the shredded chicken.

Shredded chicken:
¼ onion, coarsely chopped
1 clove garlic, sliced
1 teaspoon kosher salt
¼ teaspoon whole black peppercorns
1 pound boneless, skinless chicken breast
4 cups water

Pour water in a medium-sized saucepan and bring to a rapid boil.

Trim off any skin and fat from the chicken breast. If the breast is butterflied or double, cut in half so that the meat will cook evenly and thoroughly. Add the prepared chicken breast and all of the remaining ingredients to the boiling water, then reduce heat and simmer for 20 to 30 minutes until the chicken is thoroughly cooked. Remove from heat. Drain the liquid and discard all ingredients other than the chicken breast. With a fork or your fingers, shred the cooked chicken.

To prepare the tacos:
1 medium onion, slivered
2 tablespoons olive oil
1 teaspoon salt
Shredded chicken
Salsa de Pibil (page 56)
Corn or flour tortillas
Sour cream (optional)

In a saucepan heat the olive oil until hot, add the slivered onion, and sauté until it begins to brown and caramelize, approximately 2 to 3 minutes. Add the cooked chicken and sauté for another 2 minutes, stirring constantly to prevent burn-ing. Add the Salsa de Pibil and cook for another minute, stirring constantly to incorporate the salsa completely with the meat. Remove from heat and serve immediately with either corn or flour tortillas. Garnish with sour cream if desired.

Huevos con Chorizo
Eggs & Sausage Tacos

This is a wonderful breakfast taco, but it can be eaten at any time of day. It combines eggs with the delicious flavor of chorizo sausage. *Chorizo* encompasses several types of sausage brought to the Americas from the Iberian Peninsula (Spain). It is traditionally made from pork, although North American cooks have developed beef, venison, kosher, soy, and even vegan versions. Chorizo is classified as either *picante* (spicy) or *dulce* (mild). There are literally hundreds of regional varieties of Spanish chorizo. Both smoked and unsmoked varieties usually contain garlic, herbs, and dried, smoked red peppers, which give chorizo its deep reddish color and spicy flavor. It tends to be made from ground rather than chopped meat. This recipe uses Mexican chorizo, which is easy to crumble once you remove the casing. Though these tacos are known as a breakfast food, many Mexican restaurants in the United States and Mexico serve tacos, burritos, and *tortas* with cooked chorizo throughout the day.

²/₃ cup Mexican chorizo sausage, with outer casing removed
8 medium eggs, beaten

½ teaspoon kosher salt
Corn or flour tortillas

In a cast-iron skillet or frying pan, cook chorizo over medium to high heat, stirring constantly, for 5 minutes, until cooked.

If you have excess fat drain and then add the eggs and salt and cook until completely done, approximately 3 minutes. Remove from heat and serve immediately. I like corn tortillas with this dish, but all of my recipe tasters preferred flour.

Chicken Salad Tacos

This is a perfect quick meal for leftover cooked chicken meat. The chicken salad is scrumptious as a taco filling at dinner or as a cold salad at lunch. For a really quick meal, use a store-bought rotisserie chicken. Just pull the meat off the bones, cut it into small cubes, and combine with other ingredients. The surprise comes at the end, where I use a lettuce leaf rather than a grain tortilla. Either way they are delicious.

2 cups cooked organic chicken meat or meat
    from a rotisserie chicken, cubed
2 organic Roma tomatoes, diced
½ medium red onion, finely chopped

1 small- to medium-sized avocado, cubed
2 tablespoons organic mayonnaise
1 teaspoon chipotle en adobo
8 radicchio or butter lettuce leaves

In a medium-sized bowl, toss together onion, diced cooked chicken meat, tomatoes, and avocado. In a separate bowl, combine the mayonnaise and chipotle en adobo. Add chipotle mayonnaise to chicken mix and stir until well mixed.

Place some of the mixture inside a piece of butter lettuce or radicchio and serve.

Seafood

Fish & Shrimp Tacos

Tacos de Pescado
Fish Tacos

Tacos de pescado were popularized in Baja California, Mexico. As their name suggests, they traditionally consist of grilled or fried fish and a topping. For my interpretation on these tacos, I find that tilapia is perfect. Tilapia is a soft white fish very much like sole, and it is lean yet moist. Children love it because it doesn't taste "fishy." I love tilapia because it is a sustainably farmed fish.

Cabbage garnish:
3 cups shredded cabbage
1 teaspoon kosher salt

¼ cup cilantro, stems removed and finely chopped
1 lime, juiced
1 teaspoon black pepper, ground

Combine shredded cabbage with other ingredients in a mixing bowl and set aside until the fish is ready.

Fish:
1½ pounds tilapia fillets
½ lime, juiced
3 cloves garlic, minced
1 teaspoon kosher salt

½ teaspoon black pepper, ground
3 tablespoons olive oil
½ cup finely ground bread crumbs
Corn tortillas

Take each tilapia fillet and cut lengthwise into approximately 4-inch by 1½-inch pieces. Place them in a medium-sized mixing bowl.

In a separate mixing bowl, mix lime juice, garlic, kosher salt, black pepper, and 2 tablespoons olive oil. Pour over the cut fish fillets and toss thoroughly. Marinate for 10 minutes.

After the fish has marinated, place the bread crumbs in a separate bowl, completely coat each piece of fish with the bread crumbs, and then place it on a tray or baking sheet.

In a large cast-iron skillet, heat the olive oil over medium to high heat until hot but not smoking. Cook each fillet for 1 minute per side, or until fish is a nice golden brown color. Remove from the heat, return to the tray or baking sheet, and hold the fish in a 250° oven. Be careful not to move these fillets around too much or the beautiful breading will come off.

When all the fish is cooked, assemble the tacos and spoon a portion of the cabbage garnish on top of each fish taco. I recommend serving these tacos with homemade corn tortillas and the Tomatillo Salsa (page 57) or the Chipotle Mayonnaise (page 54).

Wild-Caught Salmon Tacos

Salmon is a favorite fish of mine, but it comes with many environmental concerns so I only buy wild-caught Alaskan salmon. The wild-caught fish has a delicious, hearty flavor and a pleasing flaky texture. Wild salmon works wonderfully when wrapped up in a corn or flour tortilla. I like to serve these tacos with Black Bean Salsa (page 58).

1 pound wild-caught salmon, skin removed and
    cut into 4 fillets
1 teaspoon salt
½ teaspoon black pepper, ground

¾ teaspoon chipotle seasoning (see Southwest
    Pantry page 60)
1 tablespoon olive oil
½ lemon, juiced
Corn or flour tortillas

Combine salt, pepper, and chipotle in a mixing bowl. Using ½ teaspoon of the spice mix, coat one side of each salmon fillet.

In a cast-iron skillet or frying pan, heat the olive oil until hot but not smoking. Cook each fillet, spice side up, for 3 minutes or until it is brown on the underside. Turn over with a spatula and cook another 3 to 4 minutes until brown. Turn over again. Top with leftover spice mix. The topside should be nicely browned in appearance. Drizzle the lemon juice over the fillets, an even amount for each. Remove from heat and serve with your favorite tortillas and salsa.

Shrimp Tacos Salpicón

The term *salpicón* means shredded or finely cut. In this case, it refers to the vegetable mixture, which is essential. Chipotle Mayonnaise (page 54) and corn tortillas complete the taco.

Vegetable mixture:
½ red onion, sliced
½ orange bell pepper, sliced into thin strips
½ yellow bell pepper, sliced into thin strips
½ red bell pepper, sliced into thin strips
½ green bell pepper, sliced into thin strips
1 teaspoon dried Mexican oregano
1 teaspoon apple cider vinegar
½ lime, juiced
1 tablespoon olive oil
½ teaspoon kosher salt
¼ teaspoon black pepper, ground

Combine all ingredients in a bowl and mix well. Set aside.

Shrimp:
1 pound raw shrimp, deveined and tails removed
1 tablespoon olive oil
½ teaspoon kosher salt
¼ teaspoon black pepper, ground
½ teaspoon chipotle seasoning (see Southwest Pantry page 60)
Corn tortillas

In mixing bowl combine shrimp with the kosher salt, black pepper, and chipotle seasoning.

Heat a cast-iron skillet or frying pan until hot. Add the olive oil then the shrimp. Sauté until the shrimp turns a bright pink color, approximately 2 to 3 minutes, stirring constantly. When the shrimp are completely and evenly done, remove them from the heat.

Spoon the cooked shrimp into a corn tortilla, top with the vegetable mixture, and top with a little Chipotle Mayonnaise. Serve immediately.

Tacos de Camarones
Shrimp Tacos

This simple shrimp taco is both fresh tasting and surprising, thanks to the spicy seasoning and fresh shrimp. I buy pink shrimp from Oregon, which are delicious and sustainable. I prefer this dish with Avocado Salsa (page 58), but you can mix and match with any salsa.

1½ lbs. uncooked, medium-sized shrimp, tails removed, deveined, and cut into three small pieces
2 tablespoons butter
2 cloves garlic, minced

½ teaspoon kosher salt
¼ teaspoon black pepper, ground
¼ teaspoon chipotle seasoning (see Southwest Pantry page 60)
Corn or flour tortillas

In a skillet over medium to high heat, melt the butter then add the shrimp pieces. Cook for 2 minutes, stirring constantly to prevent burning. Add the garlic, salt, black pepper, and chipotle seasoning and cook for another 2 minutes until the shrimp turns pink. Remove from the heat and serve immediately with tortillas and salsa.

Vegetarian

Squash, Corn & Bean Tacos

Tacos de Flor de Calabazas
Squash Blossom Tacos

Squash blossoms are considered a delicacy among some Native American tribes in the U.S. Southwest and some areas of Mexico. The male blossoms are the ones that are harvested. Their sole purpose is to pollinate the female blossoms, and they can be easily identified in a squash patch by their long stem and stamen in the middle of the flower. The female blossoms, in contrast, almost immediately lose their shape and begin to bear fruit. As long as several male blossoms are left in the squash patch, bees will be able to pollinate the female squash blossoms and the plants will produce squash throughout the summer season. I cook this tasty recipe every summer with blossoms from squash that I grow in my garden. I also buy squash blossoms at our local farmer's market. This dish is so delicious that once you try it, you will see why it was a must for this book.

1 medium to large onion, finely chopped
1 tomato, diced
1 clove garlic, minced
2 tablespoons olive oil
½ teaspoon kosher salt

¼ teaspoon black pepper, ground
16 male squash blossoms, with stamens removed
1½ cups Jack cheese, grated
Corn tortillas

In a cast-iron skillet or frying pan, heat olive oil over medium to high heat until hot but not smoking. Sauté onions and tomatoes together for 3 minutes, stirring occasionally to prevent burning. Add the garlic, kosher salt, and black pepper and sauté for 2 more minutes. Then add the squash blossoms and sauté for 1 minute, stirring constantly. Finally, add the grated Jack cheese, and cook another 1 to 2 minutes, stirring constantly until the cheese has fully melted and is thoroughly mixed with the sautéed vegetables. Remove from heat and serve immediately.

I recommend corn tortillas for these tacos as the corn nicely complements their flavor. I love to eat these tacos just as they are, although they would be delicious topped with salsa.

Mushroom Tacos

Mushrooms are the foundation of many of my favorite vegetarian meals. They have delicious flavor and texture. This recipe combines portobello, crimini, and shiitake mushrooms into a flavorful, woody dish. It is also a great accompaniment to any of the other taco recipes.

1 cup white onion, thinly sliced
2 cloves garlic, minced
2 whole portobello mushrooms, cleaned and cut
    into approximately 1-inch-long strips
2 cups crimini mushrooms, thinly sliced
2 cups baby portobello mushrooms, cut in half and
    thinly sliced

2 cups shiitake mushrooms, thinly sliced
3 tablespoons olive oil
½ teaspoon kosher salt
½ teaspoon black pepper, ground
1½ cups Jack cheese, shredded
Corn tortillas

Wash, clean, and slice the mushrooms, then set aside.

In a cast-iron skillet or frying pan, heat olive oil over medium to high heat until hot but not smoking. Add the sliced onion and cook for 2 minutes, stirring constantly until the onion is clear and starting to crystallize and turn brown. Add the garlic and cook for another minute, stirring constantly. Add the large portobello mushrooms and cook for 2 minutes, stirring to prevent burning and to ensure the mushrooms are cooking evenly. Add the crimini, baby portobello, and shiitake mushrooms and continue to cook, stirring to prevent burning, until the mushrooms are completely done, approximately 4 to 5 minutes. Add the salt and pepper, then the shredded Jack cheese and, stirring constantly, mix until the cheese is completely melted and well combined with the mushrooms.

Serve immediately with corn tortillas.

Tacos de Calabacitas con Queso Fresco
Summer Squash Tacos with Fresh Cheese

Makes 6 to 8 tacos

I love to grow Mexican squash and zucchini. The plants sprawl across my garden and provide me with a kitchen full of yellow and green vegetables. I make this traditional recipe especially in the summer months when both Mexican squash and zucchini are abundant. This simple dish will be a favorite among your vegetarian friends and family, as well as the meat-eaters. It can also be a delicious side to meat tacos.

3 medium Mexican squash or green zucchini (or combination of both), cut into ½-inch pieces
½ medium onion, chopped
2 poblano chiles, roasted, peeled, seeds removed, and diced (see Cooking & Drying Chiles page 62)

2 cloves garlic, minced
1 tablespoon olive oil
1 cup fresh or frozen corn kernels
½ teaspoon kosher salt
¼ teaspoon black pepper, ground
1 cup queso fresco, crumbled

Prepare the squashes, onion, chile, and garlic so that they are ready for the pan. In a cast-iron skillet over medium to high heat, add olive oil and heat until hot but not smoking. Add squash and cook for 3 minutes, stirring constantly. Add onion. Cook for 1 minute, and then turn heat down to low. Add the diced poblano chile and garlic and cook for another 2 minutes, stirring to prevent burning. Add the corn, salt, and pepper and cook for another 2 minutes, stirring. Remove from heat and serve immediately with crumbled *queso fresco* cheese sprinkled on top. I prefer these tacos in a corn tortilla, but they also taste good with flour tortillas.

Potato & Green Chile Tacos

This recipe is a great side dish for meat eaters or a wonderful meal for vegetarians. In Santa Fe, I can find fresh, organic produce for this recipe. I've tried using small red potatoes, fingerling potatoes, small white potatoes, and russets; they all tasted good. Potatoes are the key ingredient, so the better tasting the potato, the better tasting the dish. Organic potatoes are packed with flavor. Green chile is the other key ingredient; I recommend mild green chiles. You can always add more and different chiles to a dish to make it spicier, but you cannot take away the heat once it is there. I always use fresh chiles, but if you can't find them, you can substitute frozen or canned. I like these tacos with Pico de Gallo Salsa (page 54) or Avocado Salsa (page 58).

3 cups potatoes, sliced very thinly
2 cloves garlic, minced
½ cup white onion, diced
1 cup Roma or other heirloom tomatoes, coarsely chopped
1 cup green chiles, roasted, peeled, seeded, and chopped (approximately 4 whole New Mexico or Anaheim green chiles; see page 62 for directions on roasting your own)

3 tablespoons olive oil
1 teaspoon kosher salt
½ teaspoon black pepper, ground
½ cup shredded Jack cheese
Corn or flour tortillas

In a large cast-iron skillet or frying pan with lid, heat olive oil over medium heat and add potatoes. Sauté for 3 to 4 minutes, then add garlic. Stir to prevent burning.

Add the onions and tomatoes and cook for another 3 to 4 minutes, stirring occasionally.

Add the chopped green chiles, stir into the other ingredients, and sauté another 2 minutes.

Reduce heat to low, cover, and cook for another 7 minutes until the potatoes are cooked to the desired consistency, stirring occasionally to prevent burning. A little browning on the potatoes will give them a nice flavor and texture. Stir the kosher salt, black pepper, and shredded Jack cheese into other ingredients. Cook until cheese is melted.

Remove from heat and serve immediately with either corn or flour tortillas and your favorite salsa.

Spinach & Bean Tacos

Makes 6 tacos

This recipe is a combination of fresh spinach greens that are sautéed with cooked beans and topped with a little crumbled *queso fresco* (fresh cheese). They make a nice accompaniment to any of the meat taco recipes. I prefer organic spinach and, when I don't want to cook a pot of fresh beans, organic canned pinto beans.

1 medium Roma tomato, diced
1 sweet white onion, coarsely chopped
1 clove garlic, minced
9 ounces fresh spinach, coarsely chopped
2 tablespoons olive oil

1 cup pinto beans, cooked (fresh or canned)
½ teaspoon kosher salt
¼ teaspoon black pepper, ground
¾ cup queso fresco, crumbled
Corn tortillas

Add olive oil to a medium-sized frying pan over medium-high heat, and heat until hot. Add tomatoes, onion, and garlic and cook for 2 to 3 minutes, stirring constantly to prevent burning. Add the chopped spinach and cook for another 2 minutes, then add the cooked pinto beans, kosher salt, and black pepper. Cook for 2 minutes, stirring constantly to prevent burning.

Garnish with the crumbled cheese in your favorite tortilla. I prefer this dish with corn tortillas.

Serve immediately.

Salsas & Sides

The Secret Ingredient to Good Tacos

While the filling provides the bulk, it is the salsa that makes tacos satisfying. These brightly colored sauces give fresh and surprising flavor to every bite.

Chipotle Salsa

Makes 1 cup salsa

This salsa is easy to make and very tasty, although it does have some heat to it. If you prefer your salsa milder, add more tomato sauce to this recipe. I would increase the tomato sauce to 1½ cups, just until you build up your palate and can try this salsa in its robust essence.

2 tablespoons chipotle en adobo
1 cup tomato sauce, fresh, jarred, or canned

1 clove garlic
½ teaspoon kosher salt

In a blender combine the chipotle en adobo, tomato sauce, garlic, and salt.

Blend until smooth, approximately 2 minutes. Place in a nice salsa bowl and serve. This salsa will last for 5 to 7 days in a sealed container in the refrigerator.

Chipotle Mayonnaise

5 tablespoons mayonnaise
1 tablespoon chipotle seasoning (see Southwest Pantry)

Mix together and serve with your favorite taco.

NOTE: Store your unused chipotle en adobo in a plastic freezer bag or a container in the refrigerator for 5 to 7 days, or freeze it and use as needed.

Pico de Gallo Salsa

Makes 1½ cups salsa

This is a very typical salsa. The translation means "rooster's beak." It is a fresh condiment that is used on every taco table and typically made from chopped tomato, onion, and jalapeño and serrano chiles. This salsa may also have cucumber or even fresh radish. The longer this salsa sits the hotter is will get due to the chiles. I like to make it and eat it immediately.

5 Roma tomatoes, diced
½ red onion, finely chopped
1 jalapeño, seeds and veins removed, finely chopped
1 serrano chile, seeds and veins removed, finely chopped

3 tablespoons fresh cilantro, finely chopped
1 tablespoon fresh squeezed lime juice
½ teaspoon kosher salt
¼ teaspoon freshly ground black pepper

Combine all ingredients in a bowl. Mix together and serve. Keeps 3 to 5 days in the refrigerator.

Salsa Borracha

This salsa goes with any of the tacos in this book. Borracha literally means "drunken" and is a cooking term for recipes that incorporate alcohol. This salsa is fresh tasting and wonderful for a taco dinner, a party, or even just with tortilla chips.

½ onion, quartered
4 small or 2 medium-sized tomatoes, whole
4 jalapeños
½ teaspoon kosher salt

½ teaspoon black pepper, ground
¼ teaspoon garlic powder
¼ cup fresh cilantro, finely chopped
½ cup light Mexican beer

Using an *asador* or barbecue grill, roast the onion, tomatoes, and jalapeños until their skins are completely charred. I use kitchen tongs to turn the vegetables over the flame so that they cook evenly on all sides. Remove from the grill, place in a small bowl, cover with plastic wrap, and let rest for 5 minutes. Uncover the bowl and rinse the charred skins from the chiles. Leave the onions and tomatoes as they are. Set aside to cool.

Place the roasted ingredients (chiles, tomatoes, and onion) in a blender along with the kosher salt, black pepper, garlic powder, fresh chopped cilantro, and beer. Blend for approximately 2 minutes. Pour into your favorite salsa bowl and serve, or chill for later.

Salsa will last for 1 to 2 days in the refrigerator.

Salsa de Oregano Mexicano

This simple salsa tastes like it took hours to make—but it doesn't. The secret ingredients are the Mexican oregano, which is in the lemon verbena family, and the chile caribe.

1 cup fresh Roma or heirloom tomatoes, coarsely
    chopped
1 tablespoon chile caribe
2 cloves garlic, finely chopped

1 tablespoon olive oil
½ teaspoon kosher salt
½ teaspoon black pepper, ground
½ teaspoon Mexican oregano

In a saucepan over medium to high heat, heat the olive oil. Add tomatoes, chile caribe, and garlic, and cook for 3 minutes, stirring to prevent burning. Remove from heat and set aside.

Blend the cooked ingredients in a blender until smooth. Add the kosher salt, black pepper, and

Mexican oregano and blend all ingredients thoroughly, approximately 1 minute. Serve immediately or chill for later in the refrigerator.

This salsa will last for 3 to 5 days in a covered container in the refrigerator.

Salsa de Pibil

Makes 2 cups

This is the key ingredient for the Chicken Pibil Tacos (page 30). It also is a nice accompaniment to other cooked or shredded meats, such as pork, beef, or bison.

¼ onion, finely chopped
½ tomato, diced
2 cloves garlic, minced
2 tablespoons olive oil

1 cup tomato sauce, fresh, jarred, or canned
1 teaspoon chipotle en adobo
1 teaspoon kosher salt

In a sauté pan, heat the olive oil until hot but not smoking. Add the onion and cook for 3 minutes until it starts to caramelize. Add the tomato and cook for another 2 minutes, stirring constantly to prevent burning. Add the garlic and cook for another 2 minutes. Then add the tomato sauce, stirring to mix completely. Add the chipotle en adobo and salt, stirring again to mix completely.

Reduce heat to low and cook for another 5 minutes, stirring occasionally to prevent burning. Remove from heat, place in a blender, and blend until smooth, approximately 1 to 2 minutes. Let cool while meat cooks.

Salsa de Piña
Pineapple Salsa

Makes 1½ cups salsa

I learned this recipe from my good friend Alma, who is originally from Chihuahua. In northern Mexico, this salsa is traditionally served with the Tacos al Pastor (page 23), which are marinated pork tacos. The sweetness of the pineapple blends perfectly with the spiciness of the pork marinade; it is also delicious with chicken or shrimp tacos. This salsa has no chile, so it is sweet and perfect for people who don't care for spicy foods.

1 cup pineapple (fresh or canned), diced
    and grilled
¼ cup fresh cilantro, finely chopped
⅓ cup white onion, chopped

½ lemon, juiced (approximately 1 tablespoon juice)
½ teaspoon kosher salt
¼ teaspoon black pepper, ground

In a mixing bowl, combine the pineapple, cilantro, onion, and lemon juice. Mix well. Season with salt and pepper and serve or chill in the refrigerator.

This salsa will keep for 2 to 3 days in the refrigerator in a sealed container.

Salsa Verde
Green Sauce

Makes 1 cup of salsa

Tomatillos are sometimes called "green tomatoes," although they are not the same as green, un-ripened tomatoes. Tomatillos are a key ingredient in fresh and cooked Latin American green sauces and salsas. The ripened fruits should be firm to the touch, bright green in color, and tart in flavor.

3⅓ cups water
6 tomatillos, washed and peeled
2 whole jalapeño chile peppers, washed
3 cloves garlic, peeled and left whole
½ white onion, peeled and quartered

⅓ cup fresh cilantro, cleaned and stems removed
½ lemon, juiced
1 teaspoon kosher salt
¼ teaspoon black pepper, ground

In a medium-sized saucepan bring 3 cups of water to a boil. Add the tomatillos, whole jalapeños, garlic, and onion. Boil the ingredients for approximately 5 to 7 minutes, stirring occasionally. When done, the tomatillos will turn from a bright green color to yellow-green. The jalapeños will also turn pale green, and the onions and garlic should be soft.

Remove the ingredients from the heat, and drain and discard the liquid. Place the cooked ingredients in a blender or food processor. Add the fresh cilantro, remaining water, lemon juice, salt, and pepper. Blend until smooth, approximately 2 to 3 minutes. Pour into a serving bowl and chill in the refrigerator until ready to serve.

Tomatillo Salsa

Makes 2½ cups salsa

This salsa is made from oven-roasted tomatillos, which provide a unique flavor that is less tart than that of fresh tomatillos.

Warm water
1 pound medium to large tomatillos,
    approximately 8 to 10
3 tablespoons olive oil
1 onion, quartered
2 cloves garlic

1 fresh serrano, cut in half lengthwise and
    seeds removed
½ cup fresh cilantro, stems removed and finely
    chopped
2 teaspoons kosher salt
½ teaspoon black pepper, ground

Preheat oven to 375°.

In a medium-sized mixing bowl, soak the tomatillos in warm water with the husks on for 2 minutes. (Soaking makes the outer husk pliable.) Peel the husks from the tomatillo fruits. Cut each tomatillo

into 2 to 4 pieces, depending on size. Coat the tomatillos with the olive oil and place on a baking sheet. (I recommend lining the baking sheet with parchment paper to prevent sticking or burning.) Roast the tomatillos for 30 minutes, turning once to ensure that they cook evenly and thoroughly.

continued on next page

continued from previous page

Place cooked tomatillos, onions, and garlic in a blender or food processor and blend until smooth, approximately 1 to 2 minutes. Add the serrano, cilantro, salt, and pepper, and blend again until completely smooth, about 1 more minute.

Serve immediately or chill for later. Salsa will keep in refrigerator for 3 to 5 days.

Avocado Salsa

Makes 1 cup of salsa

Avocados add flavor to almost any taco, but they are especially good with vegetarian tacos because of the avocado's high monounsaturated fat content. When made with perfectly ripened avocados, this salsa is especially good with the Tacos de Camarones (page 40).

¼ large onion, peeled and coarsely chopped
1 jalapeño, sliced into four pieces
1 clove garlic
1 avocado, perfectly ripe
1 tablespoon sour cream
¼ teaspoon kosher salt

¼ teaspoon black pepper, ground
2 green scallions, finely chopped
2 tablespoons fresh cilantro, stems removed and finely chopped
3 cups plus 2 tablespoons water

Bring 3 cups of water to a boil in a medium-sized saucepan. Add onion, jalapeño, and garlic. Boil for 6 to 7 minutes until vegetables are soft. Remove from heat, drain the water, and set the vegetables aside.

Place avocado, sour cream, salt, black pepper, and 2 tablespoons water in a blender or food processor. Blend until smooth, approximately 2 to 3 minutes. Add scallion and cilantro. Mix together, place in a nice bowl and serve immediately.

Black Bean Salsa

Makes 1½ cups salsa

This is my favorite salsa for the wild salmon tacos but it can be used with any of the taco recipes.

¾ cup red onions, finely chopped
1 cup organic Roma tomatoes, diced
¾ cup organic corn kernels
1 teaspoon garlic, finely minced
1½ cups cooked organic black beans
1 tablespoon olive oil

1 lemon, juiced
1 jalapeño, seeds removed and finely chopped
3 tablespoons chopped fresh cilantro
1 tablespoon organic apple cider vinegar
1 tablespoon organic honey

In a medium size skillet over medium to high heat, heat the olive oil until it is hot but not smoking. Add the onions, diced tomatoes, corn, and garlic. Sauté, for approximately 2 minutes, stirring constantly. Remove from heat. In a medium-size mixing bowl, combine the sautéed ingredients with the cooked black beans and mix together. Add the lemon juice chopped jalapeño, cilantro, apple cider vinegar, and honey. Mix well. Serve immediately or chill for later use.

Freshly Roasted Sweet Corn

Makes 3 cups corn kernels

This easy roasting technique makes absolutely delicious corn. I roast a large quantity of fresh corn every summer when I can pick it at its sweetest. I scrape the cooked kernels from the cob, use some immediately, and freeze the remainder for use throughout the year.

4 ears corn in their husks
Water for rinsing plus 1 cup water

Preheat oven to 350°.

Remove the outer layer of husk, including any moldy leaves, from the corn cobs. Leave several layers of the green husk on, as they give the roasted corn kernels a delicious flavor. Immerse each ear of corn in water to make sure it is thoroughly moist. Place each cob on a baking sheet that has approximately a 1-inch lip.

Pour 1 cup water on the baking sheet and place in the oven. Bake for 10 minutes, then turn each cob and bake for another 10 minutes. Remove from oven, let cool, then peel the husks from the corncobs.

Holding each corncob upright on a wood surface or cutting board, use a sharp knife to cut downward on each cob, removing the kernels. Rotate the cob and cut again until all of the kernels have been removed. I like to reserve the cobs to make a delicious vegetable stock, but if you don't have time to do so immediately, discard them. They don't keep. Use the corn kernels immediately or freeze for future use.

Lois's Favorite Guacamole

Makes 1½ cups guacamole

I am a big fan of avocados. This recipe is very easy to make. The secret, however, is to plan your menu far enough in advance to have perfectly ripened avocados. Unripe avocados are hard and flavorless, while overripe avocados do not taste fresh. I find that store-bought avocados usually take 2 to 3 days to ripen. I have recently started to buy organic avocados because I find that they have a much better flavor.

3 small Haas avocados
½ cup white onion, diced
½ cup fresh tomato, diced
½ fresh jalapeño, seeds and stem removed, and finely chopped

1 teaspoon freshly squeezed lemon juice
½ teaspoon salt
½ teaspoon black pepper, finely ground
¼ cup cilantro, stems removed and finely chopped

Peel the avocados and remove the pits. Mash in a medium-sized bowl with a fork or potato masher. Combine all remaining ingredients in the bowl and stir to mix thoroughly. Serve immediately or cover with plastic wrap and chill for later use.

This salsa will not last more than one day and may turn a brownish color from oxidation. If this occurs, remix the ingredients in the bowl before serving.

The Southwest Pantry

Asador: A small mesh grill, also called a Santa Fe Grill by the Santa Fe School of Cooking, sold at specialty cooking stores. The grill has a stainless-steel mesh top with cast-iron sides and wooden handles. It is designed to use over the burner of an electric or gas stove. It can be used to roast vegetables such as chiles and tomatoes without burning or smoking. It is also ideal for warming tortillas. After each use, simply wipe it or brush it off.

Avocado: The avocado is a tree fruit that contains an egg-shaped pit. Cultivated in Mexico for at least 10,000 years. The word *avocado* comes from the Nahuatl word *åhuacatl,* "the fertility fruit." In Spanish it is called *aguacate.*

Chile Caribe: This is a New Mexico red chile that has been ground into small flakes, very much like the hot pepper flakes sprinkled on pizza. The flavor ranges from mild to very hot, depending on the type of chile that was ground.

Chile de Guajillo: The most common chile grown in Mexico, the guajillo is used in many sauces. It has a sweet flavor and mild to medium heat. It is sold in the Mexican food section of most markets.

Chile de Pasilla: Also known as the *chile negro,* the pasilla (Spanish for "little raisin") is a dried *chilaca* chile. This chile is dark brown, wrinkled like a raisin, and elongated and tapering. It is sold in three different grades in Mexican markets: *primero, mediano,* and the regular *pasilla,* which is what we get here in the United States. It is frequently used in moles and salsas. In California and northern Mexico dried poblano, ancho, and mulato chiles are often referred to as pasillas, but they have a different flavor.

Chipotle Chile: This large jalapeño pepper is smoked in special smokehouses, especially in the state of Oaxaca, Mexico. Much of the Mexican jalapeño crop is processed and sold as chipotle chiles. It is medium- to thick-fleshed, is smoky and sweet in flavor with chocolate and tobacco undertones, and has a very well-rounded heat.

Chipotle en Adobo: This product comes in small cans or jars. Usually, it is whole chipotle chiles that have been marinated in an adobo sauce containing onions, tomatoes, vinegar, and spices. Leftover chipotle en adobo can be frozen for future use or refrigerated in a covered container or bag for 5 to 7 days. Do not leave the chipotles in an open can as they will oxidize.

Chipotle Seasoning: This is a powdered seasoning that blends chipotle chile powder, salt, and spices. It is one of my favorite chipotle products, and I use it frequently.

Comal: A comal, which roughly translates to "cookware," is a griddle or grill typically used for cooking tortillas or foods based on tortillas, such as quesadillas. The word *comal* has its roots in the Nahuatl (Aztec) word *comalli*. The history of cooking on comales dates back to the pre-Columbian era when corn, (maize, *Zea mays*) was stone-ground, formed into tortillas, filled with whatever was available, then heated on a comal over an open fire. This technique is still used today in many parts of Mexico. The modern comal is a cast iron skillet or grill used on the stove top.

Corn Masa: This instant corn flour is made of a selected corn that is treated with lime. It is sold in almost all supermarkets and is usually found with other baking flours or sometimes in the Latino food aisle. It is sold in the same type of bag as regular wheat flour with a weight of 4.4 pounds. Masa can be used to make homemade tortillas, tamales, pupusas, atoles, empanadas, gorditas, and sopes.

Heirloom: *Heirloom* is used to describe plants that were commonly grown during earlier periods in human history, as distinct from the hybrid, sometimes genetically modified, crops used in modern, large-scale agriculture. Many heirloom vegetables have retained their traits through open pollination. Heirloom seeds are growing in popularity among gardeners as part of a movement to return to non-hybridized, ancestral seeds of historical importance.

Kosher Salt: This is the type of salt most commonly used in commercial kitchens today. It has a much larger grain size and a more open granular structure than regular table salt. It typically contains no additives, such as iodine. It gets its name because it is used in making meats kosher by extracting the blood. It gives a better flavor to foods than iodized salt does and remains on the surface of the meat longer to draw out the meat juices and enhance the flavor.

Mexican Oregano: Mexican oregano is actually closely related to lemon verbena (Verbenaceae family) and is a different plant than Mediterranean oregano. Mexican oregano is stronger and not as sweet as the oregano used in Italian cooking, well suited to the spicy, hot, cumin-flavored dishes of Mexico and Central America and perfect for chili and salsa. A highly studied herb, it is said to have medicinal properties and is commonly used by *curanderas* (traditional healers) in Mexico and the U.S. Southwest. It is available in the Mexican food aisle or the spice section of most U.S. supermarkets.

New Mexico Green Chile: This chile is the most commonly used variety in New Mexico. Its wonderful flavor makes traditional New Mexico green chile sauces and salsas distinctive. Outside New Mexico it may be referred to as an Anaheim green chile. A medium-fleshed chile, it ranges from mild to very hot. Most commonly roasted and peeled, this chile is a staple for any kitchen. Fresh chiles are available almost year-round and they freeze very well after roasting. It is commonly used for making chiles rellenos, which are basically chiles that are stuffed and fried or baked.

New Mexico Red Chile: This is the ripe form of the New Mexico green chile. It can be used in its fresh form but most commonly is strung into chile *ristras* (strings) and hung to dry. Ranging from medium to medium-hot, this chile is commonly used in red chile sauces, salsas, barbecue sauces, and as a topping for a number of dishes. It is often ground into a powder and used throughout the Southwest.

Queso Asadero: Also sometimes called *queso quesadilla,* this pale yellow or white Mexican cheese is a blend of part-skim milk cheeses. It commonly comes in a 12-ounce round package under the Cacique brand and is sold in the cheese section of most major supermarkets.

Queso Fresco: This is a light white Mexican cheese that is fresh, or uncured. It is usually found in a 12-ounce round package under the Ranchero or Cacique brand names, and is sold in the cheese section of most major supermarkets. The flavor is mild and creamy, somewhat reminiscent of a cross between cream cheese and Jack cheese.

Serrano Chile: The serrano chile most commonly sold in supermarkets is green, although it can be used in its red (completely ripened) form. A small elongated chile, it can be quite hot with a clean, biting heat. It is commonly available in the United States and used extensively in salsas.

Tomatillo: The tomatillo is also known as the Mexican tomato or ground cherry, among other names. It is a typically green fruit that is surrounded by a paper-like husk formed from the calyx. As the fruit matures, it fills the husk and splits it open by harvest time. The husk turns brown. The ripened fruit can be a number of colors, most commonly green, but also yellow or even purplish.

Tortilla Press: An essential Mexican cooking utensil, a tortilla press is used to flatten masa or wheat dough into tortillas to be cooked on a comal or cast-iron griddle. Usually resembling a round waffle iron with a flat inner surface, tortilla presses may be made of cast iron, wood, aluminum, or plastic. Look for tortilla presses on-line or in specialty cooking stores. The imported cast-iron tortilla presses are the most common and will serve you for many years. Enjoy making fresh, wholesome tortillas for your family and friends using traditional Mexican tortilla-making equipment.

Cooking & Drying Chiles

There are many types of chiles, ranging from mild to fiery hot. The degree of heat depends on where the chiles have been grown and the time of harvest—red chiles are riper than green, and as a rule taste sweeter and milder, but there are exceptions in all chiles. The variety and the growing and handling techniques will also affect the taste and heat of chiles.

Handling Chiles

Always wash fresh and dried chiles to remove dirt. Whenever handling chiles, always take precautions to avoid skin irritation: wear rubber or plastic gloves if you are sensitive to capsaicin and *do not* rub your eyes.

Roasting Chiles

There are various techniques for roasting chiles, each resulting in a slightly different flavor. Green, red, and yellow bell peppers can be roasted by the same methods. Whichever method you use, the chiles, once prepared, can be stored in plastic bags in the refrigerator for up to 1 week, or frozen and kept for up to 6 months.

The Open-Flame Method

Roast whole fresh chiles over a barbecue grill or on a gas stove with the flame set at medium high. When roasting chiles on your stove top, an *asador* is a handy tool. This apparatus fits over your gas or electric burner and has a wire mesh that the chiles can rest on while roasting. These are available at specialty cooking stores. Turn the chiles with tongs every couple of minutes until all sides are thoroughly charred.

Remove the chiles from the flame and soak them in ice water or place in a plastic bag to allow them to sweat. Under cold running water, rub the charred skins off and discard.

This method is preferable to the oven method when you are making stuffed chiles because the meat or flesh of the chile remains firm inside. If using a chile for stuffing or for cooking whole, leave on the stem and make only one slit to remove the veins and seeds, stuff the chile, and reseal it. During chile harvest season in New Mexico, large wire mesh drums are turned over an open flame and chiles roasted by the bushel and roasted chiles are widely available. For cooks in other parts of the country, check your grocer's for frozen roasted chiles that have been peeled, seeded, and chopped.

The Oven Method

Preheat the oven to 450°, place the chiles on a baking sheet, and bake 20 to 30 minutes. Turn the chiles frequently as they begin to brown until all sides are evenly blistered and browned. Remove from the oven.

"Sweat" the chiles in a closed paper or plastic bag for 5 to 10 minutes until they are cool enough to handle. Peel each chile from the tip to the stem and discard the skins. If you are drying the chiles, leave them whole at this point and continue with the drying process (described later). Otherwise, pull off the stems, remove the seeds and veins, and rinse in water to remove any stray seeds.

The Frying Method

Put 1 inch of vegetable oil in a saucepan with sides high enough to protect you from spatters. Heat until hot but not quite smoking, then gently drop in enough chiles to cover the bottom of the pan. Turn with tongs as they begin to blister. The skins will loosen as the chiles turn golden brown. Remove from the oil and drain on paper towel. When the chiles are cool enough to handle, peel the skins from the stem to the tip and discard them. Slice the chiles lengthwise, remove the seeds, devein, remove the stems, then rinse.

Drying Chiles

Green chiles can also be dried for future use, either whole or ground into powder, a technique that is especially popular in some of the pueblos of New Mexico. This drying technique was taught to my sister and me by some of the women at Isleta Pueblo.

Roast the green chiles using the oven method, then peel. Hang the chiles on a long string or lay them flat on a screen and place outdoors for about 4 days (the weather must be warm and dry). Turn the chiles daily to make sure all sides dry equally. Once the chiles are fully dried, they can be bagged and stored in a cool, dry place or ground into a powder.

To reconstitute the dried chiles, soak them in warm water for ½ hour, then remove the stems and seeds. The chiles will expand to their original size and can be used as you would use fresh chiles.

sources

This section provides a selected list of community-based companies and nonprofit organizations that publish about or sell sustainable foods. We also recommend that you support your local farmers' market for fresh vegetables, fruits, and other products.

The Cooking Post
Pueblo of Santa Ana
2 Dove Rd.
Bernalillo, NM 87004
Phone: 505-771-6752 or 888-867-5198 (toll-free)
Fax: 505-771-0392
Email: info@cookingpost.com
Website: www.cookingpost.com

Intertribal Bison Cooperative
2497 W. Chicago St.
Rapid City, SD 57702
Phone: 605-394-9730
Fax: 605-394-7742
Website: www.itbcbison.com

Native Seeds/SEARCH
526 N. Fourth Ave.
Tucson, AZ 85705
Phone: 520-622-5561 or 866-622-5561 (toll-free)
Fax: 520-622-5591
Email: info@nativeseeds.org
Website: www.nativeseeds.org

Niman Ranch
1600 Harbor Bay Pkwy., Suite 250
Alameda, CA 94502
Phone: 866-206-3327
Email: giftbox1000@bellsouth.net
Website: www.nimanranch.com

Pollo Real/The Real Chicken
Tom and Tracey Delehanty
108 Hope Farm Rd.
Socorro, NM 87801
Phone: 505-838-0345
Email: polloreal@zianet.com or info@polloreal.com
Website: www.polloreal.com

Rancho de los Garcia's
Joey Garcia
101 S. Chicago Ave.
Portales, NM 88130
Phone: 505-693-7296
Fax: 505-359-9118
Email: info@elranchodelosgarcias.com
Website: www.elranchodelosgarcias.com

Santa Fe School of Cooking
116 W. San Francisco St.
Santa Fe, NM 87501
Phone: 505-983-4511
Email: cookin@santafeschoolofcooking.com
Website: www.santafeschoolofcooking.com

Seafood WATCH
A program of Monterey Bay Aquarium intended to raise consumer awareness about the importance of buying seafood from sustainable sources.
Website: www.seafoodwatch.org

Shepherd's Lamb
Antonio and Molly Manzanares
P.O. Box 307
Tierra Amarilla, NM 87575
Phone: 505-588-7792
Email: shepherd@organiclamb.com
Website: www.organiclamb.com